Poems of Recovery
A young girl's path to recovering
from an eating disorder and amenorrhea

D1730487

boek·scout

Eerste druk © 2020 Ananda de Jager

Persoonlijke foto: © Linda Mertens - normaalgesproken.com
Illustraties binnenwerk: © Laurien Dwars (instagram @lauriendraws)
Coverfoto :   © Maria -AdobeStock
Illustraties *hartjes hoofdstukken*: © str33tcat - AdobeStock

ISBN: 978-94-640-3366-3

Uitgeverij Boekscout Soest
www.boekscout.nl

30.05.'22

ANANDA DE JAGER

Poems of Recovery

A young girl's path

to recovering

from an eating disorder

and amenorrhea

Dearest Katrin,

Hereby a little gift from my heart to yours. Never let anyone dim your light & continue to shine.

Much love,

A d'Jager

I dedicate this book to my parents.

These poems were written during a time of recovery, a time of reflection and a time where I was looking, longing, to find who I was.

My story is not what matters – what matters is that I hope people can find strength in these stories, when they see others share theirs. Life is a playground; how do you want yours to play out?

I want to thank especially my parents, for allowing me to figure out who I was and for always standing by my side, even when I was shutting you out. I want to state very clearly that nothing anyone could have done would have changed anything about my journey. This is my journey and mine to figure out.

I always say getting amenorrhea (the absence of your period) is the best thing that ever happened to me, as it taught me a lot. I would not have changed anything. I also would not have recovered from my eating disorder if my period had never disappeared.

I want to thank Anne-Wytske, Inge and Estelle, for proofreading my work. I want to thank everyone that was part of my journey, no matter how small. I just want to thank the whole world. I also want to state very clearly that these poems are about me, and not specifically about anyone else in my life.

I want to thank Mariska, for introducing me to Boekscout and giving me the faith to publish a book.

And no matter how cheesy, I want to thank myself, for always giving 100%. Sometimes it got me amenorrhea, sometimes it got me travelling around the world or publishing a book.

I want to thank YOU – for having purchased this bundle.
I hope it gives you strength.

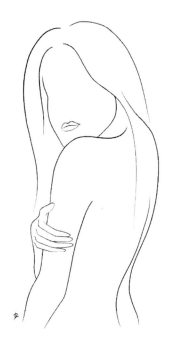

HEALING

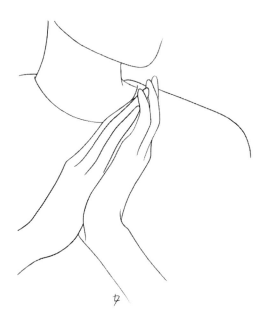

1.

One sniff was all it took

To have a totally different look

Somewhere out in space

Life suddenly did not seem like a race

Content in the here and now

I vowed to myself to take a bow

My body was capable of everything

And I have not looked back since

- *A night at the Atomium*

2.

Looking at photos of the past

I wish my thin body would last

Sucking my stomach in

Will I ever again be that thin?

- *Today I had a setback*

3.

Can a body really thrive

When it needs food to survive

And I refuse to feed it?

- *Do I want to be healthy or thin*

4.

As I lay here in bed

I often feel stuck in my head

Looking for an escape

Dying to be in a perfect shape

- *How do people eat normally?*

5.

And as I touched my skin

I realized

This is the body I will be in

This is my home

- *Take care of your home*

6.

Whatever you focus on will grow

But I want to shrink

I wish it did not show

But I need to rethink

- *The secret #1*

7.

I smiled and danced in the pouring rain

Happiness

This is what you gain

-   *Happiness*

8.

I waited for the blood to flow

But it did not show

Did I have to decide right now

That a baby could never grow?

- *Amenorrhea #1*

9.

Would I ever have a kid

Or did I ruin my body

Like god forbid

- *Amenorrhea #2*

10.

I began to see people as they are

Not skin and bones as I thought

It was me that was at war

- *It was like my vision came back*

11.

We were joking around

Even when he stood in front of me

I still did not believe it

We did not make a sound

It had been a while since then

He did not seem interested for one bit

- *It didn't even last 5 minutes*

12.

I found him interesting from the start

Some told me he once had a broken heart

I could never sense his true intention

But with the right mention

We ended up in that room abroad

And to this day I still believe it was a fraud

True, it was rather short

I guess he must have been really bored

To him it might not have seemed like much

But I had not had a single touch

There was no love to be felt

No passion to be smelled

It was a quick getting the job done

Why had we even begun?

I still wonder to this day

If I asked him again, would he stay?

-    *A one-night stand #1*

13.

And as I giggle

My thighs jiggle

- *This is life #1*

14.

If this is the storm

I decide I can handle it all

   -    *This is life #2*

15.

When I was fifteen

Eating an apple for lunch

I did not know life

Could feel like

So much love, so much a bunch

- *It gets better*

16.

If life is like a rollercoaster

I will have my ups and downs

But they will not drown me anymore

- *Recovery #1*

17.

Oh boy oh boy

I am feeling in a constant state of joy

- *Recovery #2*

18.

Never look back they say

And although I wanted you to stay

Leaving was the best I ever did

And I do not regret it one bit

- *A clean cut break-up*

19.

I stopped feeding my body

I said I'd just feed my soul

But instead of gaining life

I lost all control

- *Disordered eating*

20.

I strived for perfection I did not get

And while I'm not there yet

I am finally living again

21.

He waved at me today

And all I truly wanted to say

Is: will you come and play?

- *A one-night stand #2*

22.

I forgot what poem I wanted write

But please darling

Do take another bite

23.

I am happy

Truly madly deeply

Happy

- *I like the feeling of falling in love, so I fell in love with myself*

24.

Home.

A feeling.

My body.

My mind.

My soul.

Finally.

Home.

- *Home*

25.

Today all I wanted to do was hide

Be out of everyone's sight

And return when I am just skin and bone

I really do prefer to be alone

- *Avoiding life*

26.

She said I had more muscle

And that it looked good on me

I think I will decide for myself

Thin is what I would rather be

- *Do I want to be stronger or lose it all*

27.

I wanted to stay

In bed today

Only come out

With no weight, no doubt

- *I got up anyway*

28.

This morning,

I hated my body

This afternoon,

My colleague told me she is carrying a baby

This night,

I am amazed by what our bodies can do

- *She is carrying life*

29.

I never screamed so loud

I never felt so proud

Her body was carrying a little girl

My heart had made a little twirl

Knowing one day my body could maybe do the same

And I would be the only one to blame

If I didn't feed it

And I could never forgive myself if I did

- *I needed this reminder*

30.

The baby is the size of a kiwi now

And I stand and take a bow

No girl should ever feel the way I feel

So let's come out and be real

We are all beautiful in our own way

And I will stay

- *JOY*

31.

Recover

To be able to

Have ice cream with your daughter

Lunch with your father

Burgers with your brother

Breakfast with your mother

And if you have a son

You can tell him that you won

- *The why*

32.

And when you see your shade on the wall

And your belly looks like a giant ball

Remember that your body is trying to find peace

So breathe in, and release

- *Bloated*

33.

Can you diet your way into health?

34.

I could probably eat

Kilos of dried fig

It is myself I want to beat

Why do I allow myself to get big?

- *Binging #1*

35.

I smoked a joint today

And I should pray

Begging this disorder won't stay

Please take me away

- *How long will this last*

36.

I held my stomach

As if it had a baby in

It looked and felt bloated

Was eating really a sin?

- *I wonder #1*

37.

I downloaded Tinder once again

Hoping to find some men

Being scared to look too different in real life

What do other people do to survive?

- *Dating apps*

38.

Boy oh boy

I am overwhelmed with joy

I bought a motorbike today

And drove it all the way

To my new place

It is my fears I am trying to face

-   *Proud*

39.

Maybe we should not find joy in eating or food

Maybe we should truly focus on our mood

Find our passions somewhere else

Something that fills all our cells

Something that gives us a feeling of happiness

Something we do not need to suppress

Because by focusing on our happiness and wealth

We gain so much health

- *Finding things you love*

40.

I want to help other people

But how can I help others

If I don't know how to help myself yet?

    - *Following your own advice is hard*

41.

I danced around the room naked today

Finally free, you would say

See,

We all have our ups and downs

But if you only give frowns

The world will give them back to you

So dance,

It's all you should really do

-   *Rhythm of life*

42.

My thighs touched this morning

And I am trying to remember

What I have to gain instead of

What I want to lose

I had cake with my parents

A lunch with a friend

Dinner with my grandma

Will these feelings ever end?

If people judge you based on your looks

They should really be out of your books

- *You gain life*

43.

Maybe we should all just accept

Being perfectly

Imperfect

44.

I read a story today

And the woman, she would say

The effect restricting had on her body

And I will spill the tee

It was not pretty

She has issues with her gut

And for her period, no blood

Her body turned into shock

Because you see,

A body is not hard like a rock

Your hormones get messed up

And not only that,

On top

You lose yourself and maybe some friends

And when you think it never ends

Another issue might pop up

Only you can make it stop

Take care of your body like it is your baby,

And maybe, just maybe

Someday you will be free

-    *I believe I can be free*

45.

Poem forty-five

I ain't nobody's wife

I downloaded Tinder

But I let love hinder

Not sure if I am ready to fully open up

Or do I just want to open my top?

-   *Mixed feelings*

46.

If all your body is trying to do is survive

Can you really thrive?

We might need more food than we actually think

Maybe just let that sink

Your body is like a smart machine

Unlike anything you have ever seen

Machines need care as well

So do not be surprised when I tell

Eat a little extra with your meal

It is truly not such a big deal

- *Thriving #1*

47.

When I was fifteen,

It is myself I wanted to punch

When I was sixteen,

I had an apple for lunch

And I didn't think at twenty-five,

I still had to deal with this entire bunch

- *Stop before it's too late (also, it's never too late)*

48.

Someone just ate a bag of chips before lunch

Why would you eat a whole bunch?

He has a weird eating pattern I see

Is that who I was also destined to be?

I decided to take faith in my own hand

And truly mend

The broken patterns in me

I decide that is who I was destined to be

-   *Destiny #1*

49.

I didn't think it would help this much

To be fully out of touch

With the people whom did me wrong

I guess I did turn out strong

But I must admit and not forget

All the things done and said

I was also to blame

Not just him as I claim

- *When two people fight, there's two to blame*

50.

I kept myself in that relationship

And if I could give my younger self one tip

It would be to not fear the unknown

If you know you've outgrown

The person you once loved so much

There will be another person to love and touch

-   *End it when you feel it is over*

51.

I truly did my best

To give my body some rest

I guess one day was not enough

But working out less was tough

Until I just couldn't do it anymore

And constantly felt sore

I would drag myself to the gym

Only to be super slim

When the focus shifted to being strong

I realized I treated my body very wrong

How do you recover from something so deep

When your body is so tired, even the stairs seem too steep?

- *Exercise addiction*

52.

They tell you they wished they had your motivation

To go to the gym six times per week, that is determination

Little did they know

And it clearly did not show

That my body was never rested

And that I just had gotten tested

To see if my hormones were okay

I lost my period already once

So I wonder if it will stay

- *There is a lot behind the surface that people do not see*

53.

Every day I ask myself

Who do I want to be?

- *Myself*

54.

I want to heal my relationship with food

I want a period, with blood

If that means my jeans won't fit

Maybe that will just be it

I will buy a new pair of jeans

Because by all means

My body should not adjust to my clothes

Even if buying a bigger size blows

- *Acceptance*

55.

As if a body is something you can just adjust

-   *Change your perspective*

56.

My jeans are getting tighter

But my eyes are shining brighter

My thoughts are getting lighter

I always knew I was a fighter

- *Fighter*

57.

I feel the pressure of my belt on my skin

Why did I decide not to be stick thin?

- *Recovery is hard*

58.

Writing helps to let go

Even if sometimes it goes slow

I hate to pause and take a break

Can't I just be healed for god's sake?

- *How long does it take*

59.

I drink no more skinny teas

I eat more than just a few peas

My hips shake like never before

But I still want to work on my core

Maybe some things will never fade

And in summer I prefer to hide in the shade

If I learned only one thing

It's that in this life, we should sing

-   *Did this poem even make sense*

60.

A drop here and there

Drawing a circle in a square

It's the stupid things that count

Not whether you added a pound

- *Nobody cares about your weight gain*

61.

Hair as thin as ice

Falling out, like no surprise

Always being stone cold

And not listening to what you are told

Seeing the fear on your parents' face

Still making weight loss a race

The struggle inside your head

Only quiet when you go to bed

Forcing yourself to workout

Thinking you will make yourself proud

But baby girl look what you did

Ruining your body in the process to get fit

- *Amenorrhea #3*

62.

I would love to do the same diet as before

But I know deep in my core

If I would go back to restricting

And let me tell you it's conflicting

That I would put it all back on

As if I had never begun

Can somebody please tell me the way out

So I can truthfully feel proud

Or will I feel like this all my life

Just me, trying to survive

- *I wonder #2*

63.

A belly round as a ball

A lover to catch me before I fall

A dog, a swing and my own place

Lingerie, made of lace

The room ready for a baby girl

A ring with a lovely pearl

Maybe fairy tales do come true

Now I just need to meet you

- *Dreaming of the one*

64.

Many words left unspoken

Never knew I was still broken

How long does it take to truly feel good

Instead of wanting to spill blood

I do not want to give my body any food

I want to be stick thin

And then when I commit a sin

I would be like the devil, just skin and bones

They say words hurt more than sticks and stones

But the pain I feel inside

I cannot force to hide

Can someone please take me away

Because I really don't want to stay

I want to escape from this life

Always just trying to survive

The feelings just keep coming up

Can someone please make it all stop?

- *Relapse #1*

65.

I let it out

I cried it through

I cried it out

I let it through

I let it cry

I cried

- *Crying*

66.

Am I really so much more human

With more than just flesh on my bones?

- *All feelings came up*

67.

I squatted fifty-five kilos today

And every day I would wonder

Do I want to be strong or skinny

What gives me my thunder?

- *Choices*

68.

Maybe I should just believe

That I can have it all

The body, the passion, the mind

Nothing would make me fall

If I truly believed in the possibilities

I could stand up so tall

- *The secret #2*

69.

In life, you do not just get what you deserve

So if someone is getting on your nerve

Try to remember you attract it all

Even the 3am phone call

-    *The secret #3*

70.

The higher you vibrate

The more conscious your state

The better will be your flow

So are you ready to let the old stuff go?

- *Abundance*

71.

Did you ever have a fear so deep

That anytime you wanted to take a leap

Something would pull you back

And bring you off track

It feels you take many steps

But somehow you relapse

-   *Relapse #2*

72.

Hearing someone say it out loud

Does not at all make me proud

Why can some girls be fit and thin

While eating out and drinking gin

Having a period every 4 weeks

Without any little tweaks

I want to have it all

But instead I break and fall

My body has to recover now

It feels all my fault somehow

How your mind can play a trick

And make your own body sick

What if I can never have a kid

Just because of some stupid diet I did

Do I choose life or do I fall

I just want to have it all

- *Have it all*

73.

I saw the pain in my parent's eyes

To me it came as a surprise

I looked fit and thin and had reached my goal

I was totally in control

Gave my hundred percent

An eating disorder they could not prevent

- *Control*

74.

Writing a few poems a day

Can still not make the pain go away.

75.

Have to eat it all

Have to eat it all

Maybe I stand up tall

My jeans do not fit at all

I have to eat it all

I have to eat it all

- *Binging #2*

76.

My jeans feel tight

They just don't fit right

My body is not a home anymore

And taking care of it feels like a chore

All I ever wanted was a strong core

But now all I can think is

Eat more

- *Where is the limit*

77.

First they said you look so fit

No belly, even when you sit

Then they said you got too thin

Where did it even begin?

People wonder now how I can eat so much

But I have just completely lost touch

To feel what my body needs

To know on what it feeds

What is a normal eating pattern?

Will my stomach ever again flatten?

- *Normal eating*

78.

Meal prep they say

Your hunger will fade away

A glass of water before the meal

Will really do the deal

Sports to keep you fit

Move even if you sit

Change the way your body looks

So you can be perfect in the books

When actually you're ruining it inside

And there is no way anymore to hide

Sticks and bones was all you were

Do you really want to go back there?

- *Conversations with myself*

79.

They say I look just fine

That weight gain happens with time

I don't believe in the laws of aging

So instead, I keep on raging

The war against the way I look

Until the disorder overtook

Was it really just about the smaller stomach

Or was there something else to sum up?

- *I wonder #3*

80.

Does it really matter what you look like

Or is it more about the energy you carry inside?

81.

What do you want to be remembered for?

For being a bore?

Never taking that extra bite

Always putting up a fight

Feeling guilty about food

Will never do anyone any good

So maybe you want to be remembered for other skills

Not for being a skeleton dancing on pills

But rather for the energy you had

Or how you lift up someone when sad

For the love you were able to share

Life can be so beautiful when you care

Because trust me little girl

This world will make your head twirl

Eating disorders are a true fight

And recovery never seems to be just right

So let's have one last look back

And keep going on the right track

Fight your demons off

Be true to you, be tough

Be remembered for the great things you achieved

Not for what you believed

About bodies having to be a certain shape

Using food as an escape

When you truly let go of all your fear and control

You will honestly finally feel full and whole

82.

To the little girl in me

I'm not who you thought I would be

I thought at twenty-five,

I might be someone's wife

That I would be free of all fear of food

And truly feel good

See this is the skin

That for the rest of my life I will be in

Why did I treat my body so wrong for all these years

And create many food fears?

Now all I can do is fight to overcome

And be who I was destined to become

- *Destiny #2*

83.

When I read about women over thirty-five

Who have lived most of their life

Worrying about food

Not being understood

I decide I do not want to live like that

Even though weight gain might feel bad

In the end, my body will find its peace

Allowing me to finally release

All the pain I kept inside

Let us shine finally, bright

- *Recovery #3*

84.

A bloated belly on top

Eating I cannot stop

I open up my pants

Touch my belly with my hands

All I truly want is a real hug

Maybe I can shake off this feeling with a drug

Not sure how to deal with this alone

Being bloated around my skin and bone

- *I swear my body is under this bloated one*

85.

I faced my fears and hired a food coach

I hope this is the right approach

86.

What works for you

Might not work for somebody else

See, we are not all the same

No one is to blame

- *Stop comparing*

87.

Eyes wide open and bright

The little girl just lost sight

Some more restriction here and there

Suddenly you are in too deep to share

Thought it would go over with age

This destruction is like a cage

Had I known when I was fifteen

I would not have been so mean

Destroying my own body

To be thin for anybody

We are ten years later now

And all this time did I never allow

Myself to eat enough

To be healthy, strong and though

This time I have to make it through

If not for me, then for you

- *I do it for the kid inside of me*

88.

Little girl, don't cry

Little girl, don't be shy

Little girl, try try try

Little girl, don't cry

- *Cry*

89.

To my twelve year old self

Be yourself

To my thirteen year old self

Don't try to halve

To my fourteen year old self

Don't leave half the food on the shelf

To my fifteen year old self

Don't eat all the food from the shelf

To my sixteen year old self

Love yourself

To my seventeen year old self

Love yourself

To my eighteen year old self

Love yourself

To my nineteen year old self

Love yourself

Love yourself

Love yourself

- *Love yourself*

90.

What if you are thirty-one

And you still don't dare to eat a bun

What if you are thirty-six

And you never eat a Twix

What if you are thirty-nine

And you are still scared to shine

What if you are forty-two

And you eat so much you forget to chew

What if you are forty-eight

And you still want to lose weight

What if you are fifty-three

And in your mind you are still not free

What if you are sixty-five

And you never truly lived your life

What if you are seventy-seven

And all you want is to have peace in heaven

Suddenly you are eighty-nine

Had you chosen recovery

Your whole life would have turned out just fine

- *Choose recovery*

91.

There is a voice inside my head

It tells me not to eat, but rather go to bed

There is a sound inside my soul

That only has on goal

To be thin as ice

Some people do not have this noise

But I do hear this voice

I go against her every day

Will she ever go away?

- *Recovery #4*

92.

I decide I dislike the word recovery

As if there is something wrong with me

Apparently, I have a mental health issue

But there is no dream I cannot pursue

I am not my illness

I choose to be my wellness

I turn it around

If you are not lost, how can you be found?

- *Wellness*

93.

They say my body needs rest

That I put it too much to the test

Who are they to decide I overtrain?

Wasn't the motto 'no pain, no gain'?

I think my body has superpowers

I can work out for hours

- *I am invincible*

94.

I believe I am right

And I will not go down without a fight

I will prove them all wrong

Because I am strong

They are just jealous that I am skin and bones

While I can eat all the scones

The fact that I am cold all the time

And my skin does not shine

Does not mean a thing

As long as I am thin

Bodies do not need to rest

When I train, I am on my best

I know what is right for me

So just let me be

- *Denial*

95.

I finished the whole peanut butter jar

I didn't have to go so far

But it felt so damn good

To finally be able to eat all the food

My body needs the fat

And my mind a reset

- *Binging #4*

96.

I have the same lunch for two years

It does not bring joy, it brings tears

I have had the same breakfast for two years

It does not bring joy, it brings tears

I used to eat only an apple for lunch

Never go out for brunch

I start a new meal plan tomorrow

I am ready to let go of all the sorrow

- *Letting go*

97.

Change is scary you see

But I am not who I used to be

I do not want to live like this all my life

Pretending to survive

So I take a leap of faith

Why wait?

- *Faith*

98.

In every second
Every minute
You can make choice

In every second
Every minute
You can raise your voice

In every second
Every minute
You can raise your joys

In every second
Every minute
You can play with toys

In every second
Every minute

You make the choice
- *I choose happiness and abundance*

FEELING

99.

This is a fresh start

I feel proud, I feel smart

I document the process

To remind myself not to be less

To take life with all that it brings

And my heart

My heart silently sings

- *Silently sings*

100.

The highest vibration is joy

A child playing with a toy

A mother with her child

Dancing in the wild

Singing on the top of your lungs

Kissing with tongues

Yes

The highest vibration is joy

- *And boy, do I choose joy*

101.

Hundred poems further now

And I finally allow

Myself to invest

Put my fear to the test

Switch up my eating game

No more guilt and shame

-   *No more guilt and shame*

102.

My binging was at its peak

Last week

I watched videos on attracting what you are

The more I showed my scar

The bigger it became

You attract things that are the same

So I made hundred-eighty degree change

No more pains

Multiple intentions per day

I am here to stay

- *I choose to stay*

103.

You cannot change the past

But you can be at your best

By changing the memories you have

Focus on what made you laugh

Release any blockage you created

Let go of whom you hated

And create a new past

Only keeping the best

- *Let go, let go, let go*

104.

I lie in bed with a smile on my face

Life is not anymore a race

My soul learned its lesson this week

And with a little tweak

Life looks much brighter now

- *Now*

105.

To my daughter I will say

Please do not be afraid to stay

Stand up tall and proud

Making mistakes is allowed

Love your body as it loves you

Cherish the moments,

There are only a few

Compliments are free,

Give them away

Give love to people,

Always continue to play

To my daughter I will say

Love yourself, it's okay

-   *It's okay*

106.

If I ever have a day off again

I go back to my writing

And remember then

All the good things this life has

Despite me having been a mess

- *Still learning*

107.

Find your passion

Do what you love

Learn your lesson

Be soft and tough

Focus on your goal

Do not care what other people say

There is no such things as control

Focus on you and be okay

- *Do what you love*

108.

A belly as round as a ball

But I continue to stand up tall

In it for the long run

So might as well have some fun

Bloated I might be

Not like anyone will now see

I will continue to find my peace

At my own pace

- *At my own pace*

109.

Life might sometimes be tough

But I keep my spirits lifted

I keep my spirits up

- *Lifted*

110.

I let go of my old blocks

Anything that is holding me back

It might come in waves and shocks

But I'm right on track

- *On track*

111.

People who I thought were confident

And competent

Revealed that they were insecure

And I was just not sure

How people are so beautiful and tough

Judged themselves so rough

And then I thought to myself

Aren't you doing the same to yourself

- *Judging yourself*

112.

There is a big smile on my face

And oh by god's grace

You came into my life

When I just wanted to survive

Last night you stayed

Not sure if you played

But I could truly feel the joy

Oh boy oh boy

- *I could truly feel the joy*

113.

Safe and secure

Naked and pure

My fingers following your spine

All is fine

- *All is fine*

114.

A step into the new

Only a few

Feeling a little bit in love

This road will not be tough

Everything just feels right

With you by my side

- *With you by my side*

115.

I want to go to bed

But a song plays inside my head

A song of love you see

A song about you and me

- *Love song*

116.

Was last night a one-night stand?

Why did it have to end?

Will we meet again one day?

Or is it a game you play?

Everything felt so good

You were totally in the mood

My hand in your hand

I know you through a mutual friend

Is it a hookup or more

I do feel it in my core

This story is not finished yet

So I will try again, to go to bed

-   *Questions in my head*

117.

If happiness is a choice

I will keep raising my voice

I will choose it over and over

Be my own lover

I will let my light shine

Be mine be mine be mine

- *Be myself*

118.

When we were laying in the bed

And suddenly you said

Don't expect too much

I felt like losing touch

Why did you say it so soon

I don't want to be over the moon

Let's just see how it goes

Because whatever flows, flows

-   *Feelings*

119.

Maybe I am not enough

Or you want to act all tough

You want things to move slow

And this triggers me to a new low

But I will face every trigger I get

And continue to hug you in bed

I should first be enough for me

And then we will see

Self-care is priority number one

So for now we won't be done

- *Not just yet*

120.

Happy

Happy happy

Happy

I have never been this

Happy

- *Happy*

121.

My emotions are going all the way

I am okay

I am okay

My emotions are going all the way

I am not sure I can handle it today

- *Not today*

122.

Baby, the higher your ups

The deeper your downs

But wear it with pride

Like a crown

- *Pride*

123.

Eat a bit more they said

Don't feel hungry when you go to bed

With the food came also the feeling

I guess it's part of healing

I'm not sure I can handle it all

Would someone pick up if I call?

Isn't it easier to just go back

Weigh my food, keep track

Just to not feel so much

Or does it mean feeling out of touch

You see,

I do wish to be free

From my disordered thinking

But today I just feel like sinking

My emotions are too much for me to handle

Can we hug in front of the light of a candle?

- *I don't want to be a burden*

124.

I tell my friends they don't have to do it alone

Tell them how much they've grown

But when I need help myself

I go back into my shelf

Pretend I can do it, just me

But there's a lot more strength in we

We don't have to do it alone

Look at how much we have grown

-   *Asking for help*

125.

He cancelled a few times

Now I'm trying to write rhymes

To keep my thoughts of things

How can other people have easy flings?

My emotions are like a rollercoaster

I don't want to put bread in the toaster

This poem makes no sense

But in my defense

Neither does my mind

Or am I just blind

- *Overthinking*

126.

They ask me if I want to go back to being stick thin

As if it was a sin

They ask me if I would go back there

Feeling thin as air

The truth is that I would

It doesn't mean I should

Now I have pancakes on a Saturday afternoon

And maybe saying yes to going back was too soon

I am dancing on the street of joy

Going back there would be like playing with a dangerous toy

- *But I like playing*

127.

Do I want to date someone

Who cancels 50/50

He might be the one

But it is too risky

- *Risky*

128.

The first time he had to reschedule

I felt rejected and dull

The second time was a bit more okay

I still wondered if he would stay

The third was expected

I felt rejected but connected

The fourth was just annoying

Made me wonder if he was toying

So do I really want to sign up for this

Afraid of what I otherwise might miss?

-    *Choose yourself baby girl*

LIVING

129.

I avoid my family

Because they confront me

They see it all

When things don't go well, I don't call

I want to hide away

There is a true fear to stay

- *Stay anyway*

130.

As I reflect upon the year

I feel no doubt, I feel no fear

I have done all that I could

Faced all my fears with food

And just fell so damn good.

As I reflect upon the year

I feel no doubt, I feel no fear

I am content with what I have done

Now it is time for some fun

- *Fun*

131.

The progress between you and me is still slow

I am doing my best to make it flow

Sometimes I hit an all-time low

There are many things I want to say

I am scared you will not stay

But life is like a play

So I take my power back

Bring myself on my own track

This is not an attack

I only want people who care to be in my life

Been spending long enough to survive

Now it is time to thrive

- *Thriving #2*

132.

Everything happens for a reason

Just like each season

Sometimes it might feel like you are stuck

Remember you are not a rock

You create your own space to grow

Just let life flow

Focus on your goals

Hang out with beautiful souls

Somedays you will feel the blues

But you create your own rules

- *You create your life*

I AM FREE

Poems of recovery

Is a collecting of poems

About finding oneself during

The process of healing

The relationship with food

Not only that,

When you work on loving yourself

There is a lot more you gain in return

Life <3